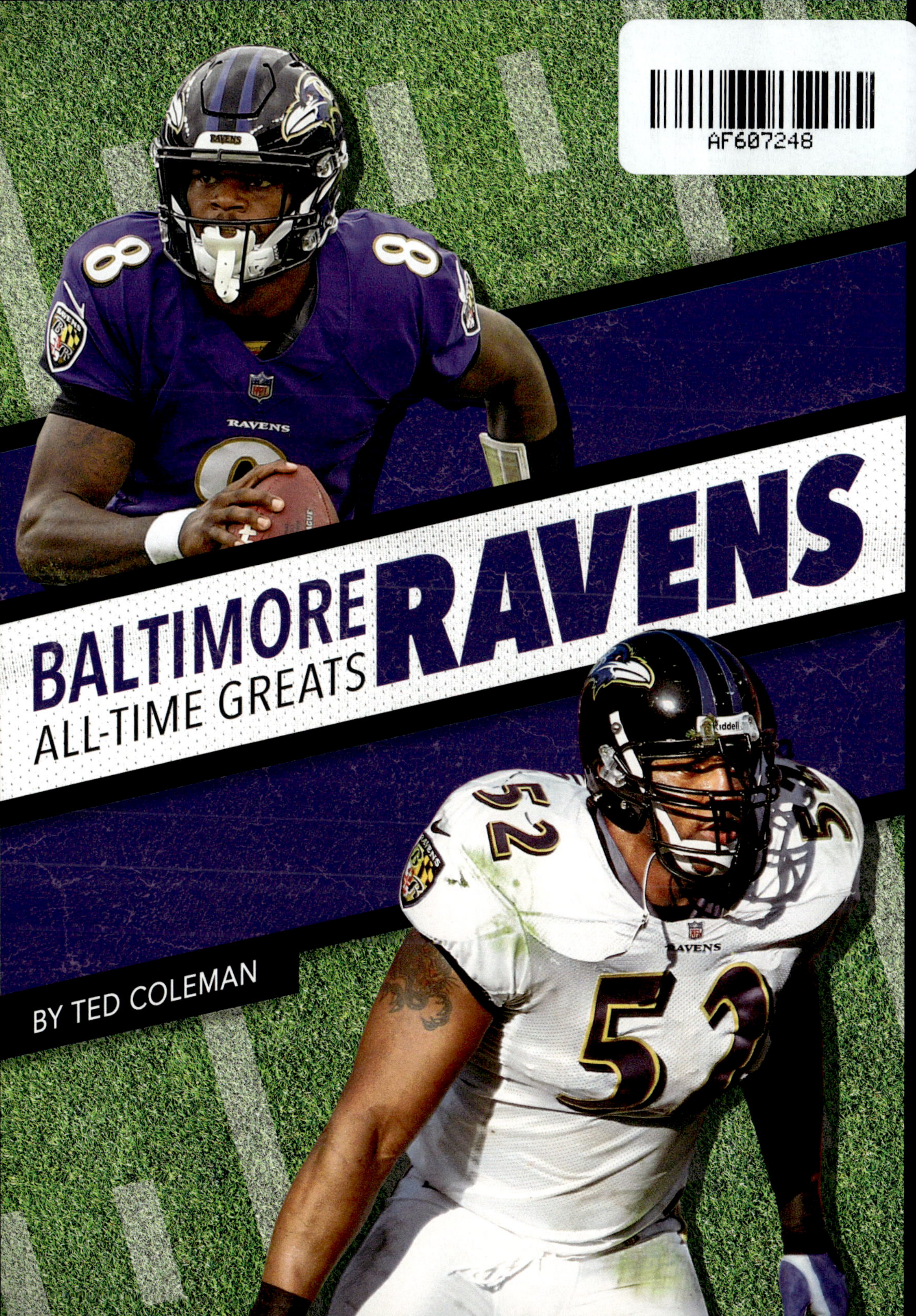
AF607248
BALTIMORE RAVENS
ALL-TIME GREATS
BY TED COLEMAN

Book design by Jake Slavik
Cover design by Jake Slavik

Photographs ©: Nick Wass/AP Images, cover (top), 1 (top); Kevin Terrell/AP Images, cover (bottom), 1 (bottom); Rob Carr/AP Images, 4; G. Newman Lowrance/AP Images, 6, 8, 10; Gene J. Puskar/AP Images, 13; Paul Spinelli/AP Images, 14, 17; Gail Burton/AP Images, 18; Scott Boehm/AP Images, 20

Press Box Books, an imprint of Press Room Editions.

**ISBN**
978-1-63494-352-9 (library bound)
978-1-63494-369-7 (paperback)
978-1-63494-402-1 (epub)
978-1-63494-386-4 (hosted ebook)

**Library of Congress Control Number: 2020952625**

Distributed by North Star Editions, Inc.
2297 Waters Drive
Mendota Heights, MN 55120
www.northstareditions.com

Printed in the United States of America
082021

# ABOUT THE AUTHOR

Ted Coleman is a sportswriter who lives in Louisville, Kentucky, with his trusty Affenpinscher, Chloe.

# TABLE OF CONTENTS

LEWIS
52
RAVENS
52

## CHAPTER 1
# TOP DEFENSE

After the 1995 season, the Cleveland Browns moved to Baltimore. But the Browns left their name and history behind. The Baltimore Ravens made a fresh start in 1996.

In the team's first draft, Baltimore chose a pair of future Hall of Famers. Offensive lineman **Jonathan Ogden** made 11 Pro Bowls in a row from 1997 to 2007. During his long career, Ogden blocked for several great Ravens running backs.

Meanwhile, linebacker **Ray Lewis** brought a fierce intensity to the team's defense. He won two Defensive Player of the Year awards. Lewis

helped make the Ravens defense one of the best in the National Football League (NFL).

**Peter Boulware** joined Lewis at linebacker in 1997. He racked up 11.5 sacks that season. He also earned Defensive Rookie of the Year honors. Boulware and Lewis formed one of the league's best linebacker groups.

Up front, the defensive line featured **Michael McCrary** on the end. McCrary joined the team in 1997. He and Boulware became Baltimore's top sack specialists.

By 2000, the Ravens had built one of the greatest defenses of all time. But the team's offense struggled to score points. During one stretch, the Ravens went five straight games without scoring a touchdown. Fortunately, they could rely on kicker **Matt Stover**. He was one of the most accurate kickers in NFL history.

## BRIAN BILLICK

As an assistant coach, **Brian Billick** was known for leading great offenses. For example, he led the Minnesota Vikings offense in 1998. That team set a record for scoring the most points in NFL history. Billick became the Ravens' head coach in 1999. His teams quickly became famous for defense. The Ravens had a top-10 defense in eight of Billick's nine years as coach.

The 2000 Ravens won the Super Bowl thanks to their great defense. But they did have a couple bright spots on offense. Rookie running back **Jamal Lewis** posted 1,364 rushing yards. It was just the start of a great career with the Ravens. In 2003, Lewis became the fifth player in NFL history to rush for more than 2,000 yards in a season.

Quarterback **Trent Dilfer** didn't have great stats during the 2000 season. But he avoided big mistakes. And with such an amazing defense, the Ravens didn't need an elite quarterback. Dilfer played just one season in Baltimore. But the defense stayed together for years.

STAT SPOTLIGHT

**CAREER RUSHING YARDS**

RAVENS TEAM RECORD

**Jamal Lewis: 7,801**

HEAP
86

# CHAPTER 2
# A SECOND TITLE

Tight end **Todd Heap** joined the Ravens in 2001. He just missed the team's Super Bowl run. But he learned from a man who'd been there. **Shannon Sharpe** was one of the best tight ends in NFL history. Heap became an outstanding tight end himself. He was a great receiver who could also block well.

**Derrick Mason** was the Ravens' other big receiving threat. Mason became Baltimore's all-time leading receiver. He was also reliable. Mason didn't miss a single game during his six seasons with the Ravens.

In 2002, the Ravens drafted safety **Ed Reed**. By the late 2000s, he had become one of the top safeties in the NFL. Reed was known as a ball hawk. Each week, he spent hours studying films of opposing teams. He knew exactly where to be to intercept the ball.

Linebacker **Bart Scott** also joined the Ravens in 2002. He was speedy and could play all over the field. With Scott and Ray Lewis, Baltimore had two of the best linebackers in the league. But the duo broke up after the 2008 season. Scott signed with the New York Jets.

STAT SPOTLIGHT

**CAREER INTERCEPTIONS**

RAVENS TEAM RECORD

**Ed Reed: 61**

REED
20

SUGGS
55
RAVENS
55

The Ravens had another star linebacker in **Terrell Suggs**. Suggs earned Defensive Player of the Year honors in 2011. And the following season, the Ravens made it back to the Super Bowl. Ray Lewis and Ed Reed were both playing in their final seasons with Baltimore.

**Haloti Ngata** anchored the defensive line. Ngata was huge and strong. He could shut down a running play all by himself. On some plays, he even threw offensive linemen back into the quarterback.

## JOHN HARBAUGH

**John Harbaugh** was a surprise choice to lead the Ravens in 2008. He had never been a head coach in the NFL. But he proved he was up to the job. He took the Ravens to the playoffs in each of his first five seasons. In the fifth, he won the Super Bowl. In 2015, Harbaugh became the winningest coach in Ravens history.

The 2012 Ravens had one major difference from the 2000 Ravens. This time, the team featured a great quarterback. **Joe Flacco** had been with Baltimore since 2008. He was the team's all-time leading passer by his third season. Flacco threw for an impressive 3,817 yards in 2012. But he was at his best in the playoffs.

Flacco didn't throw a single interception in the playoffs. In the Super Bowl, he passed for 287 yards and three touchdowns. Flacco won the game's Most Valuable Player (MVP) award. More importantly, the Ravens won a second title. Flacco played six more seasons with Baltimore. By the time he left, he held all the team's major passing records.

FLACCO
5
RAVENS
5
Wilson

JACKSON
8

CHAPTER 3

# THE NEXT WAVE

Offensive lineman **Marshal Yanda** protected Flacco for 11 years. Yanda made eight Pro Bowls before retiring in 2020. By that time, the next great Ravens quarterback was on the rise.

Quarterback **Lamar Jackson** transformed the Ravens into a team known for its offense. Jackson was a great passer and an outstanding rusher. In 2019, he ran for 1,206 yards. That was a new NFL record for most rushing yards by a quarterback. Jackson took home the league's MVP award that year. His exciting style of play earned him plenty of fans around the NFL.

The Ravens hadn't completely forgotten about defense, though. Tackle **Brandon Williams** was a mean presence on the line. His aggressive tackling and strong arms put fear into quarterbacks around the league.

On special teams, the Ravens once again had an elite kicker. By 2019, **Justin Tucker** was the most accurate in NFL history. In his first eight seasons, he made 90.8 percent of his field goal attempts.

The only problem for the Ravens was the playoffs. Despite Jackson's amazing first two seasons, he hadn't won a playoff game. That changed after the 2020 season, when Jackson notched his first playoff victory. Ravens fans hoped it was only a matter of time before the team brought home another Super Bowl trophy.

## C. J. MOSLEY

Baltimore drafted linebacker C. J. Mosley in 2014. The Ravens hoped Mosley would be the next Ray Lewis. By 2018, Lewis himself said Mosley was the best middle linebacker in the NFL. Mosley made the Pro Bowl in four of his first five seasons. But Mosley didn't get the chance to match Lewis's legacy with the Ravens. He signed with the Jets in 2019.

# TIMELINE

1996
JONATHAN OGDEN
(1996–2007)
RAY LEWIS
(1996–2012)
PETER BOULWARE
(1997–2005)
SHANNON SHARPE
(2000–01)
BART SCOTT
(2002–08)
TERRELL SUGGS
(2003–18)
MARSHAL YANDA
(2007–19)
2010
JOE FLACCO
(2008–18)
JUSTIN TUCKER
(2012–)
MATT STOVER
(1996–2008)
MICHAEL McCRARY
(1997–2002)
2000
TRENT DILFER
(2000)
JAMAL LEWIS
(2000–06)
TODD HEAP
(2001–10)
ED REED
(2002–12)
DERRICK MASON
(2005–10)
HALOTI NGATA
(2006–14)
BRANDON WILLIAMS
(2013–)
C. J. MOSLEY
(2014–18)
LAMAR JACKSON
(2018–)
2020

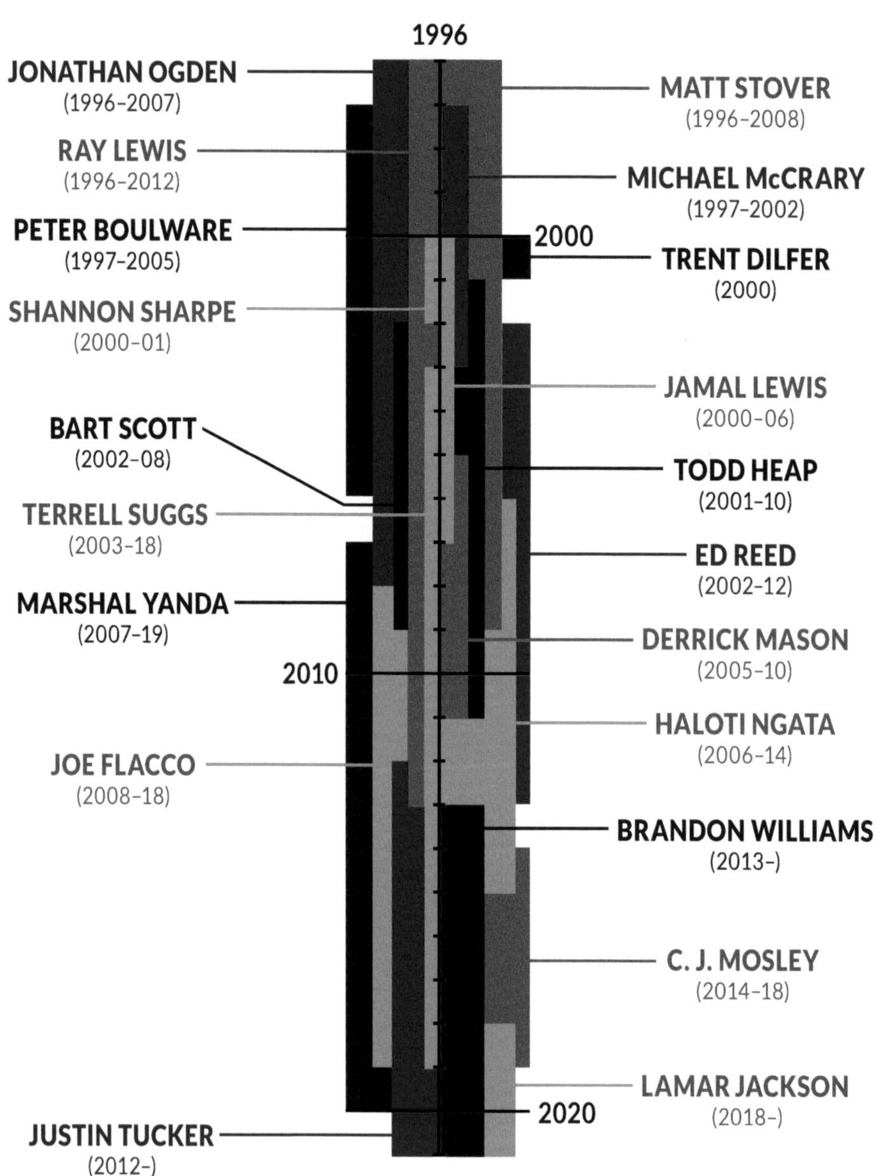

# TEAM FACTS

## BALTIMORE RAVENS

**Founded:** 1996

**Super Bowl titles:** 2 (2000, 2012)*

**Key coaches:**

**Brian Billick** (1999–2007), 80–64–0, 1 Super Bowl title

**John Harbaugh** (2008–), 129–79–0, 1 Super Bowl title

### MORE INFORMATION

To learn more about the Baltimore Ravens, go to **pressboxbooks.com/AllAccess.**

These links are routinely monitored and updated to provide the most current information available.

**1966 through 2020*

# GLOSSARY

**draft**
An event that allows teams to choose new players coming into the league.

**elite**
One of the best.

**linebacker**
A player who lines up behind the defensive linemen and in front of the defensive backs.

**Pro Bowl**
The NFL's all-star game, in which the league's best players compete.

**rookie**
A professional athlete in his or her first year of competition.

**sack**
A tackle of the quarterback behind the line of scrimmage.

# INDEX